I0709642

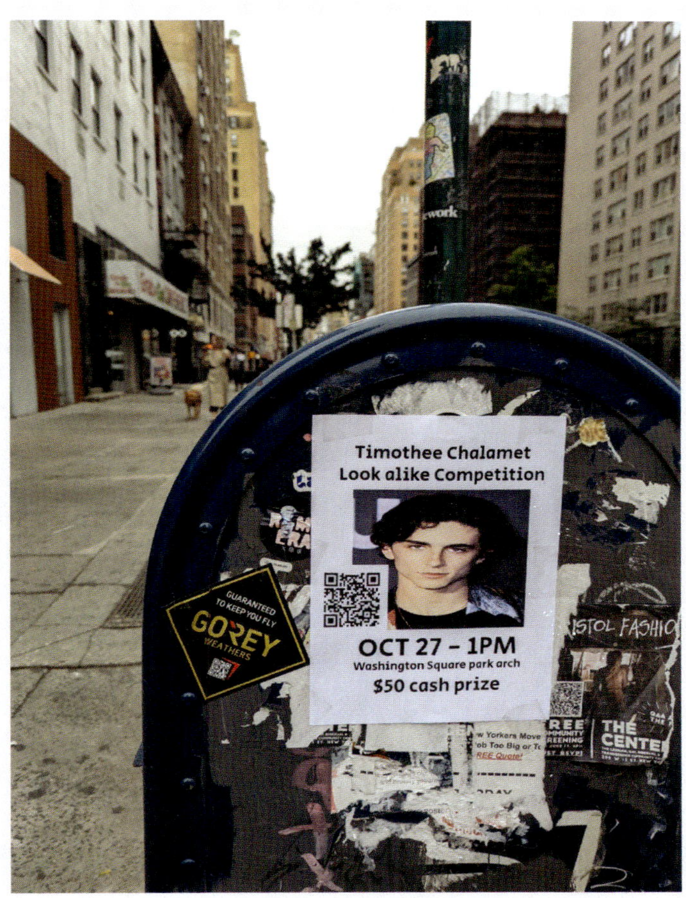
Timothee Chalamet
Look alike Competition
OCT 27 – 1PM
Washington Square park arch
$50 cash prize
GUARANTEED
TO KEEP YOU FLY
GOREY
WEATHERS
ISTOL FASHIO
THE CENTER

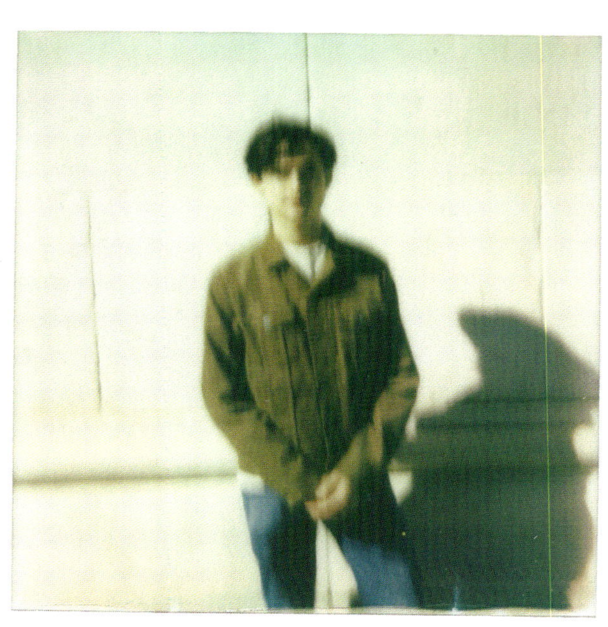

I'm Timothée.

You're Timothée.

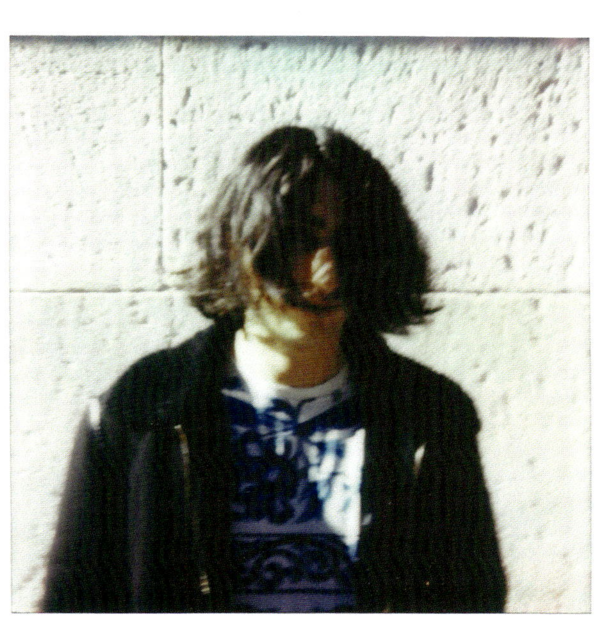

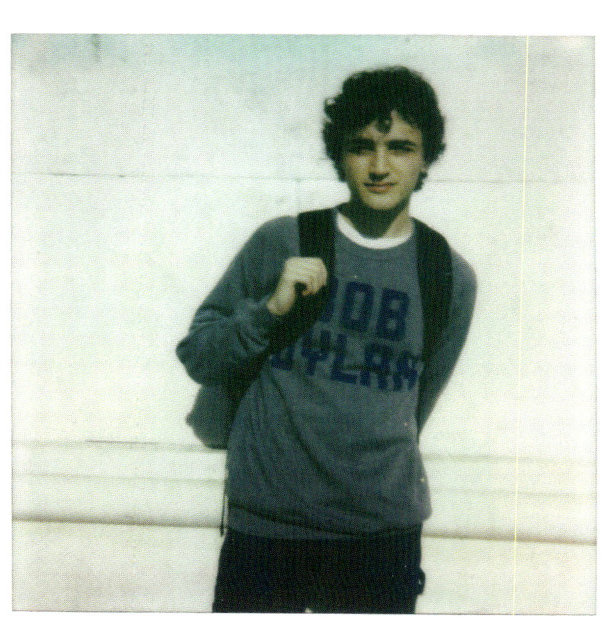

We're all Timothée.

— as said by an attendee

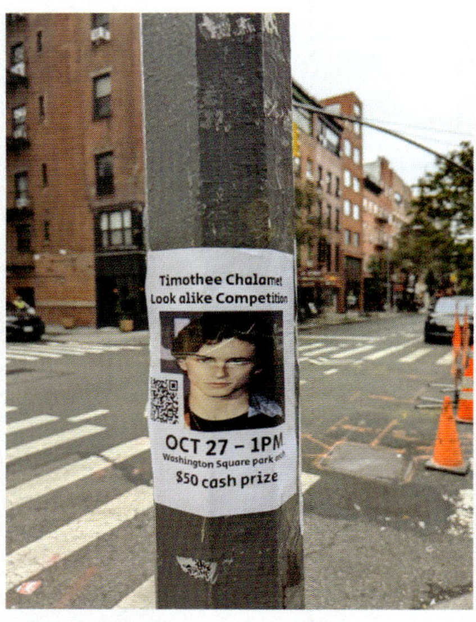

Timothee Chalamet
Look alike Competition
OCT 27 – 1PM
Washington Square park arch
$50 cash prize

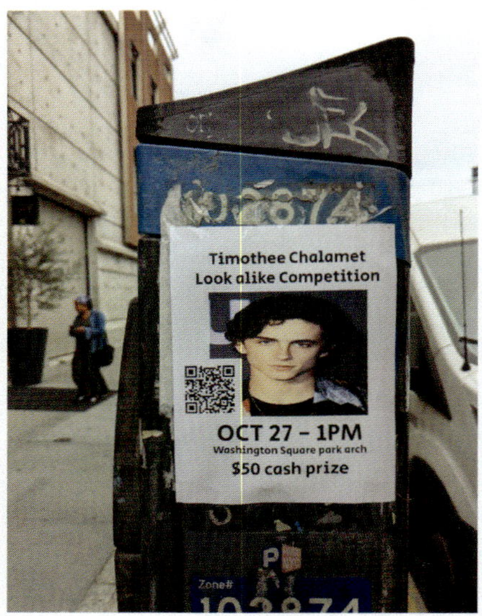

Timothee Chalamet
Look alike Competition
OCT 27 – 1PM
Washington Square park arch
$50 cash prize

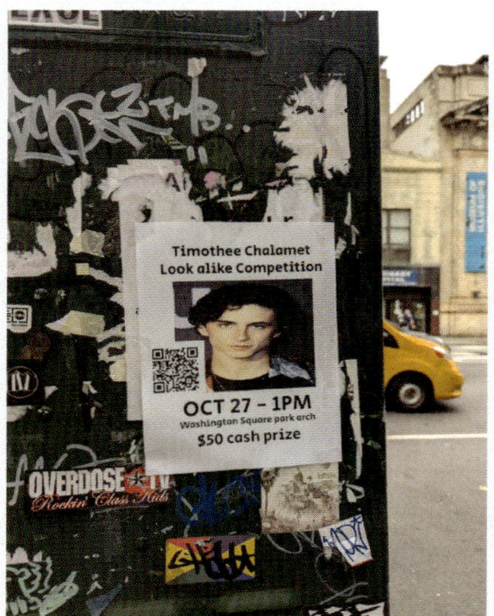

Timothee Chalamet
Look alike Competition
OCT 27 – 1PM
Washington Square park arch
$50 cash prize

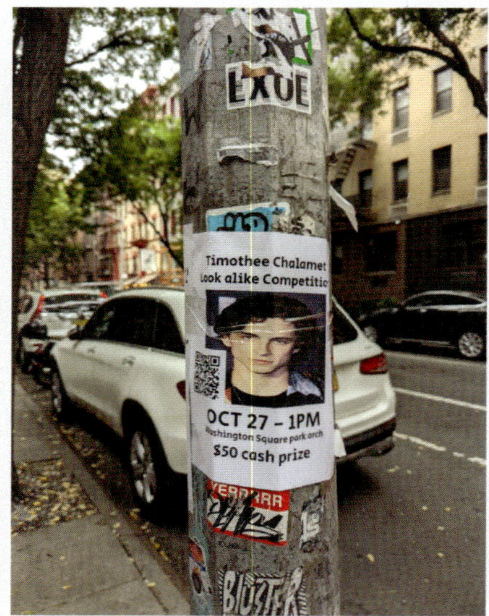

Timothee Chalamet
Look alike Competition
OCT 27 – 1PM
Washington Square park arch
$50 cash prize

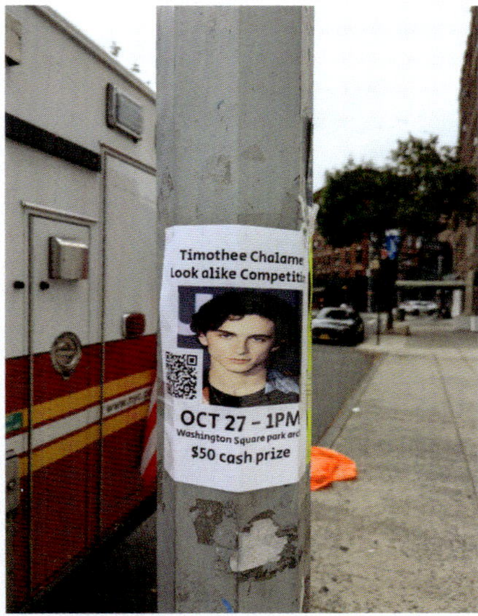

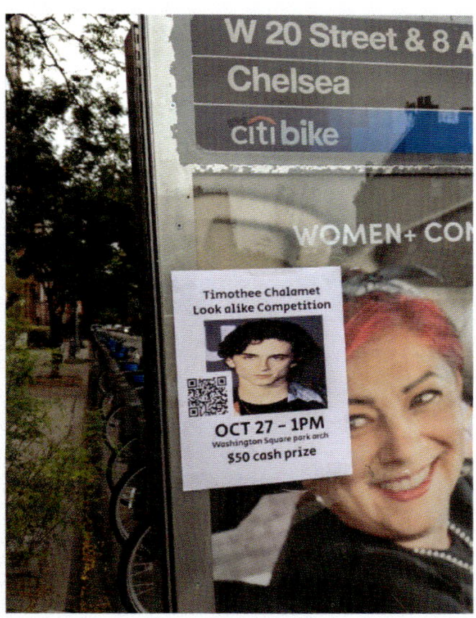

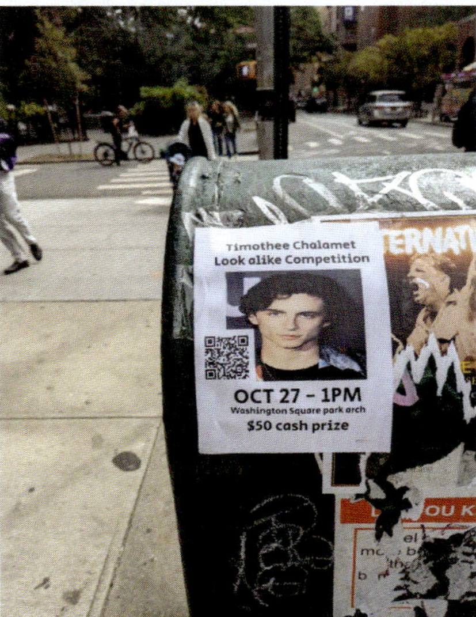

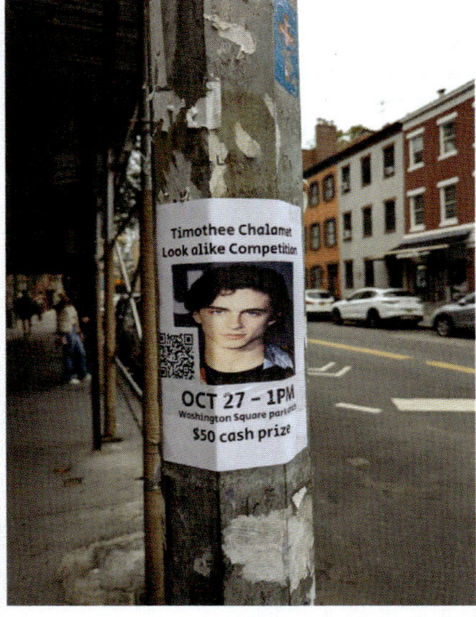

Images courtesy Anthony Po

Call Me Timothée

The Timothée Chalamet
Look-Alike Competition

Jonathan Hollingsworth

Blurring Books

October 27th, 2024, 1:00 p.m.
Washington Square Park, NYC

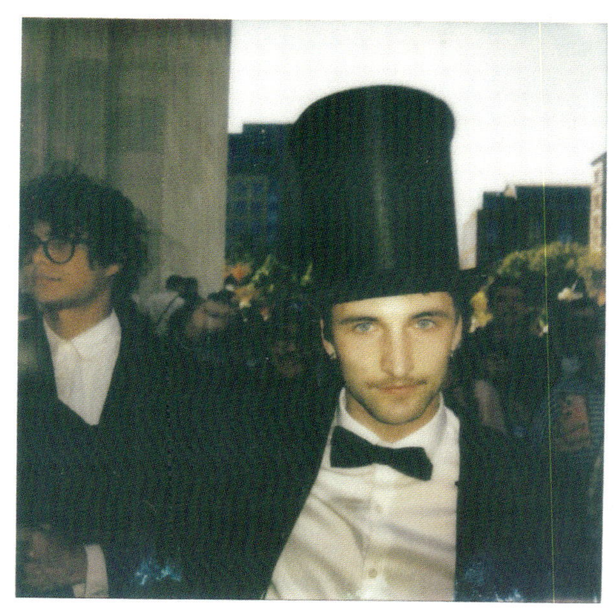

Anthony Po

Q & A with Anthony Po, Organizer of the Timothée Chalamet Look-Alike Competition

JONATHAN HOLLINGSWORTH: *How did you land on the idea of doing a Timothée Chalamet look-alike competition?*

ANTHONY PO: I've been in love with hanging up posters for dumb events. And we knew a Timothée Chalamet look-alike competition would get really big. I also look like Timothée Chalamet.

Considering your substantial following, why did you make the choice to host the event under the "Gilbert" pseudonym? Was there a greater power in anonymity?

People don't like to be marketed to. If I were to have hosted it under my brand, it wouldn't have got as big, I guarantee it.

When you conceived the competition, how did you think it would go? And how did it exceed expectations?

We knew it was gonna be big, but we didn't know how big. We're really happy that we didn't get arrested. We had a full contingency plan ready in case I did get arrested.

Given the enormous turnout and bonanza of media coverage, your idea clearly struck a nerve and captured the zeitgeist. What do you think the buzz and hoopla say about where we are as a culture?

I think people yearn for whimsical things. The world can be far too serious and money-motivated. I will continue to provide these things as long as there is a need for them in the market.

For most of us there, Timothée Chalamet's arrival was a little like Godot making a surprise appearance. I don't think anyone imagined it would happen. What was that next-level moment like?

It's funny, we would've put money on the fact that he wouldn't have shown up. But I think, ultimately, from a PR perspective, it was the best thing for him to do. I just hope he had fun and he sells a couple more tickets.

I got a summons and a $250 fine (and I didn't even host the event)! What did the NYPD have to say to you? And what were your repercussions?

Luckily, I had my bodyguard accept the tickets under his name. Obviously, I'm paying it though (ha ha). My producer had leaked an email before and they sent us a cease-and-desist and that was the only reason we ended up getting the fine in the first place. The park, they don't want us to have fun (ha ha).

After Cheeseball Man and Chalamet, where do you go from here?

I'm gonna keep hosting events. I actually have a boxing match against the supervillain named "Cornhead Killer" on the 16th of November. I've been training pretty much every single day for it.

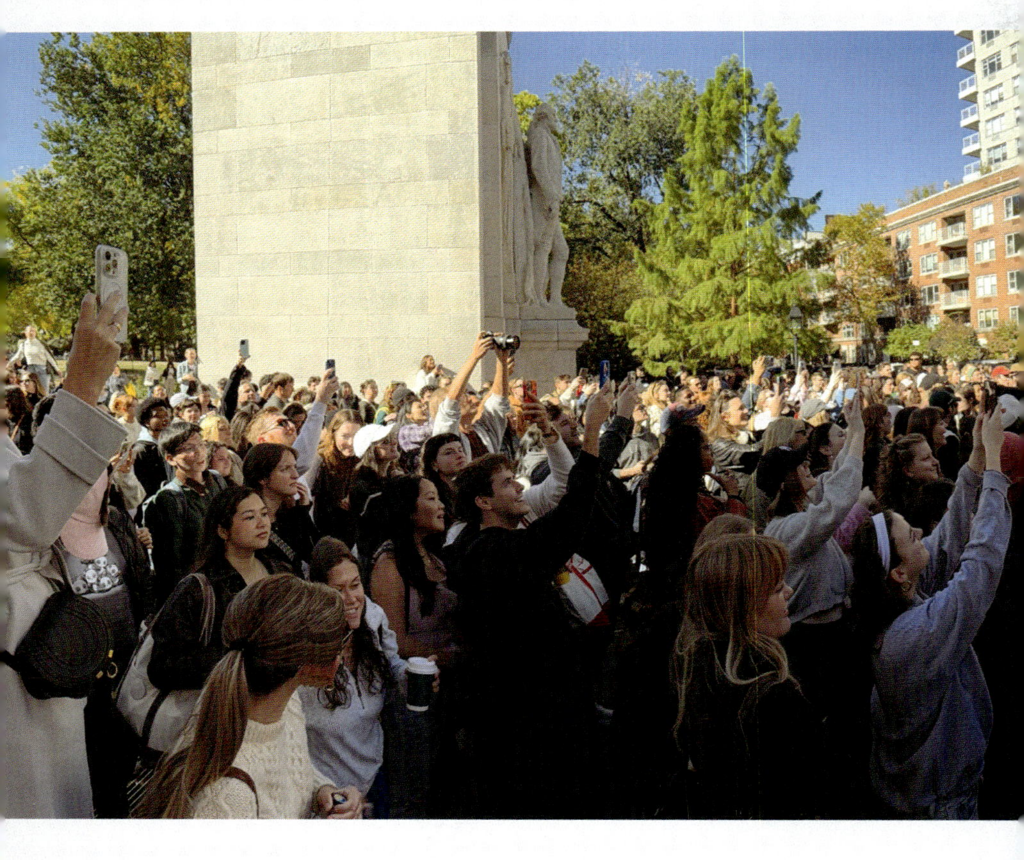

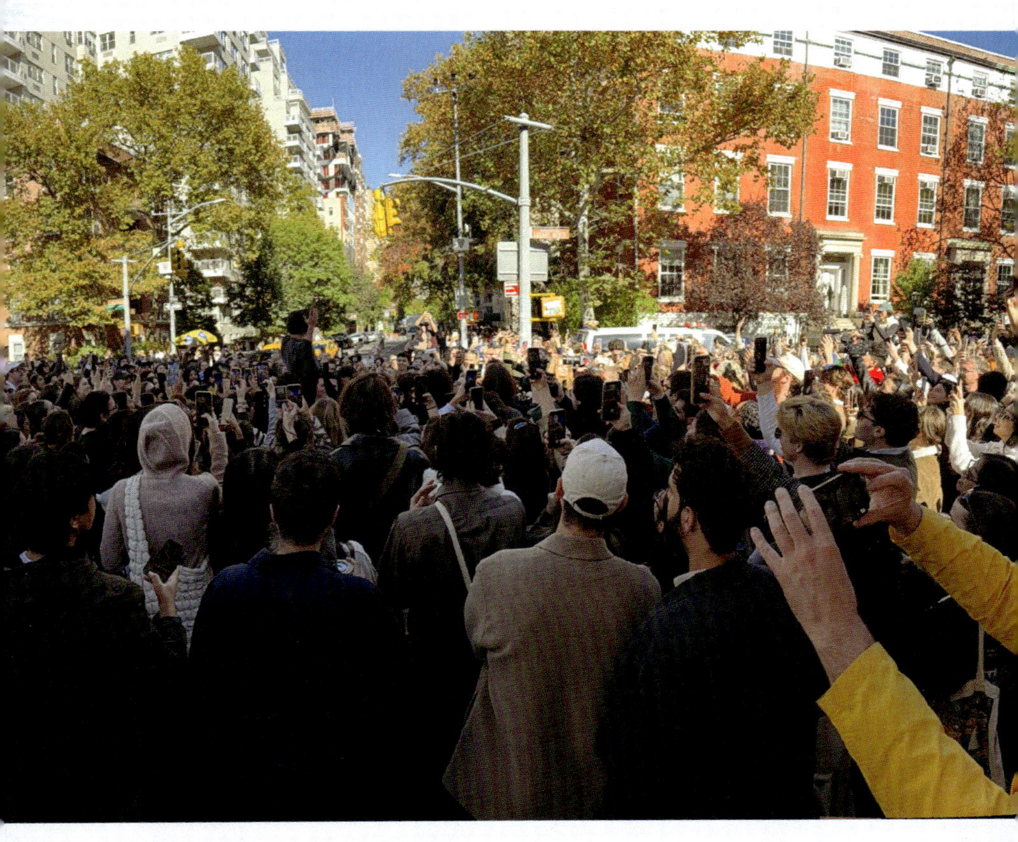

Washington Square Park by Stefan Shanni

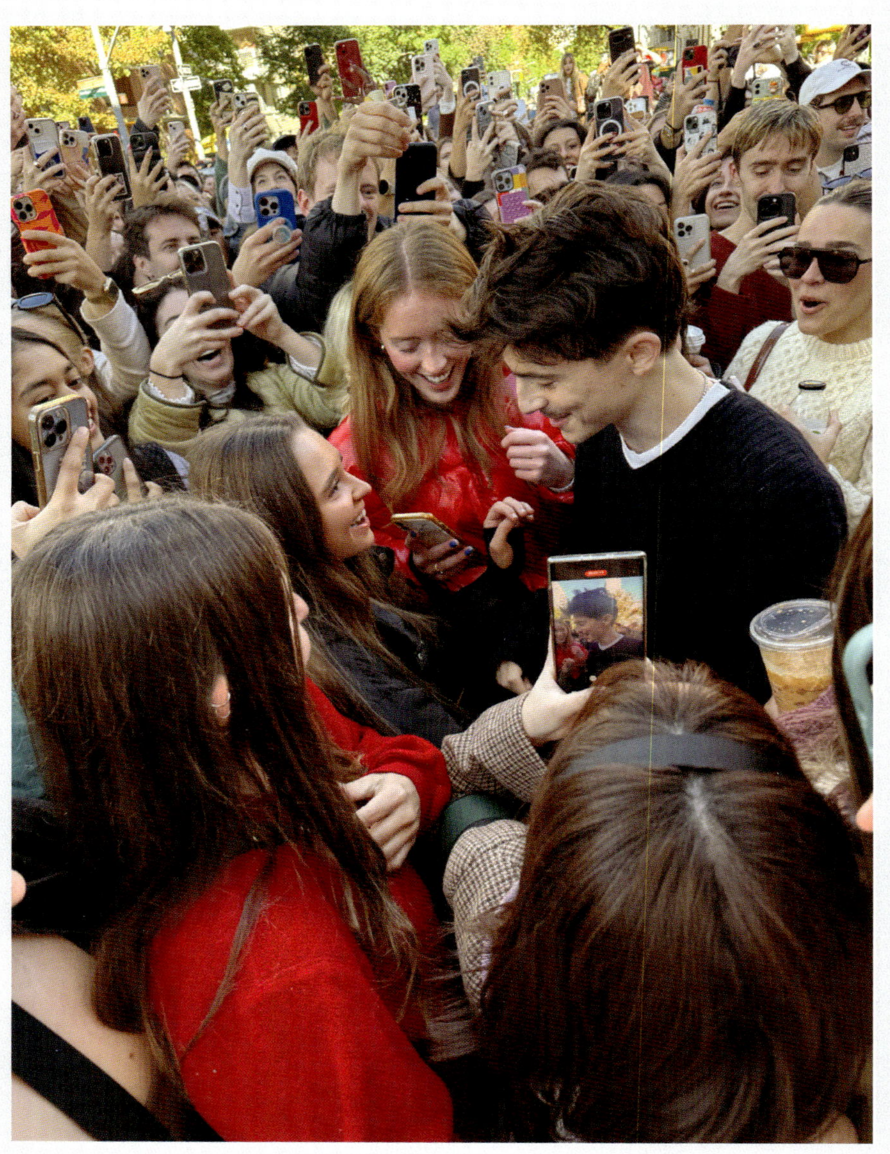

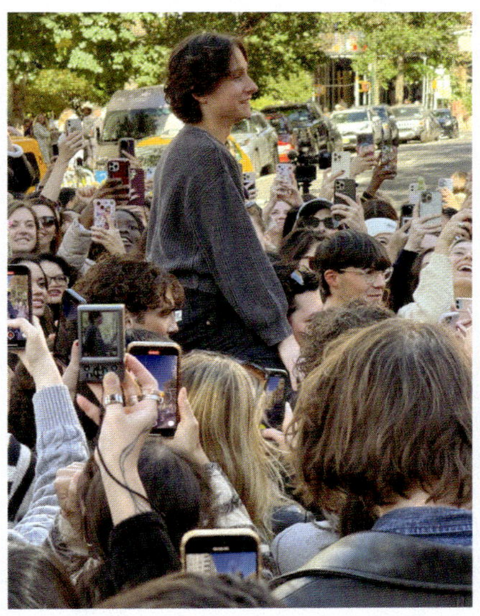
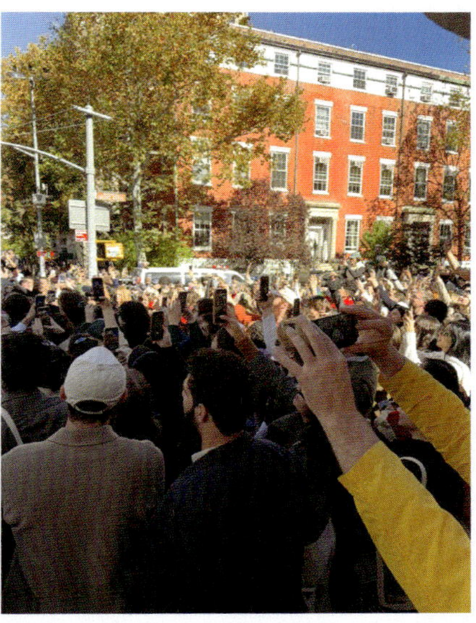
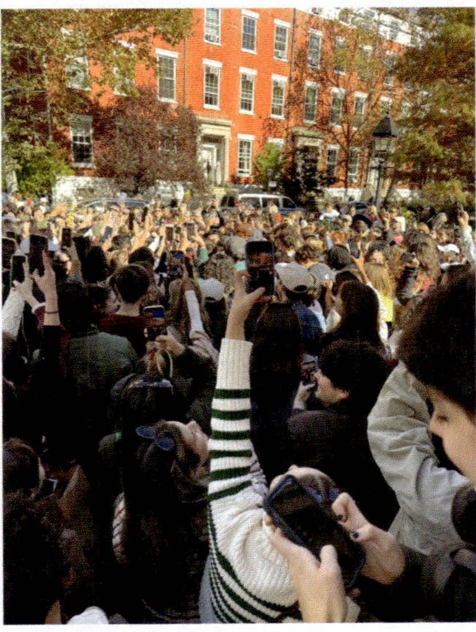
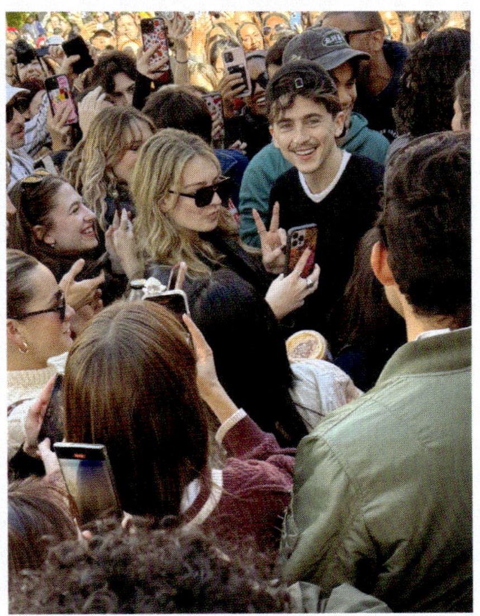

Images by Stefan Shanni

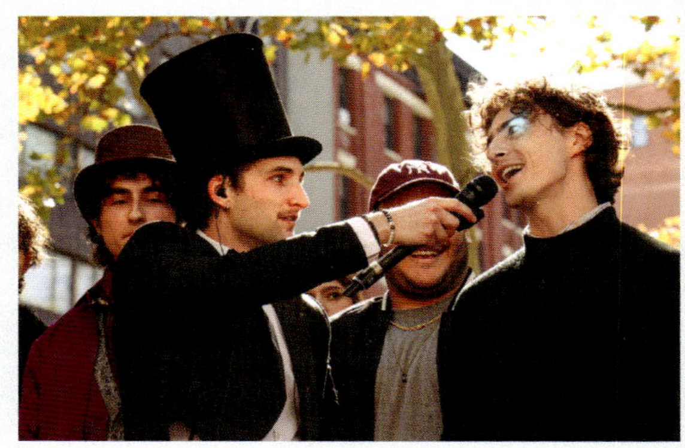

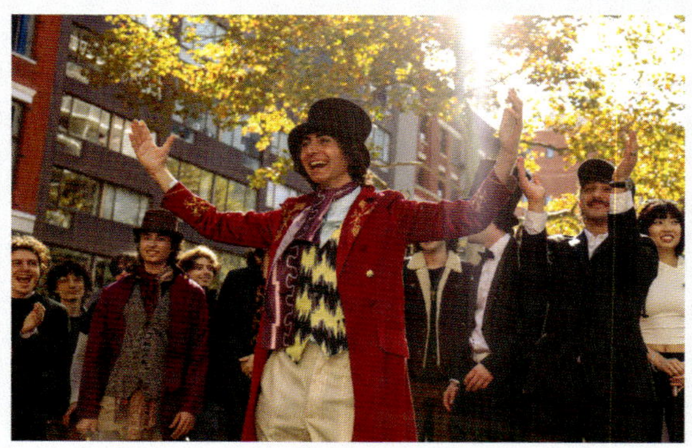

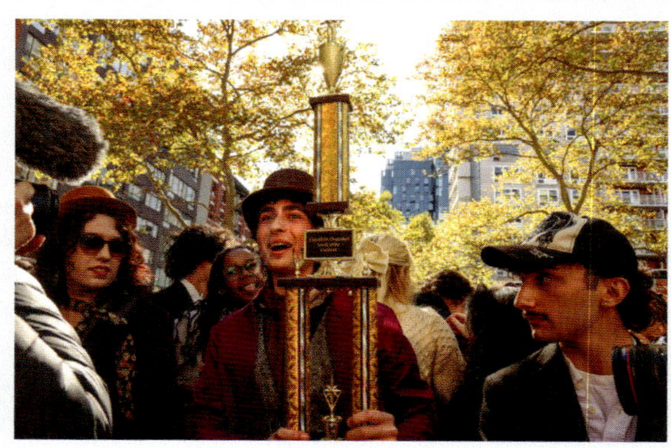

Images courtesy Julia Smerling

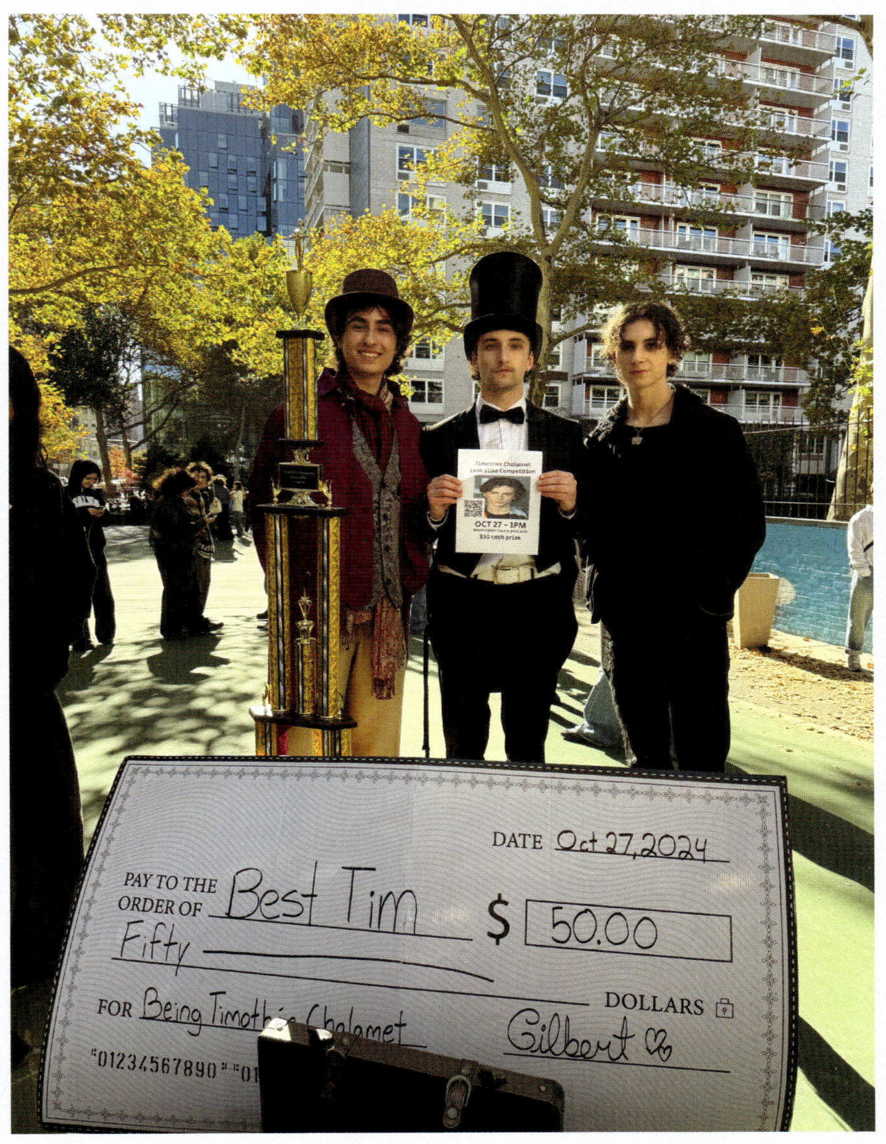

Image courtesy Anthony Po

Miles Mitchell, 21, of Staten Island (left) wins "Best Tim" and a $50 prize, pictured beside organizer Anthony Po (center)

About the Pictures

I read the news of the competition during some late-night scrolling, the kind that isn't conducive to sleep. A Timothée Chalamet look-alike competition was the perfect amusement to roll off the assembly line of the fun house of our cultural moment. It promised to be ridiculous, and fun, and of course I would be there in what was a pleasant distraction from a fraught election cycle.

Maybe it was the strobes and umbrellas that got me in trouble. Or the generator and white seamless paper taped to the base of the arch in Washington Square Park, where Harry had once said goodbye to Sally. Five humorless NYPD officers — to be fair, just doing their job — approached with pointed questions about what I was doing, while sussing out whether I'd organized the event. A summons and $250 fine followed, with the offer of a second if the equipment wasn't dismantled and packed up, stat.

Fortunately, I brought my Polaroid and the packs of film that were veterans of my frightening refrigerator, but by that time, hundreds of people were in Washington Square Park, and whatever initial ambitions I had for my pictures went *poof*. The media and Timothées were there, too; some bouncing on shoulders, throwing their hands in the air to the cheers of the crowd.

And then the real Timothée arrived, dressed just like one of us. The light changed, the air grew thin. Every phone was raised — tapping, tapping — in orbit around him. And then, before the crowd could grow bold and cut locks from his hair or tear a swatch of his clothes, the seas parted and Chalamet was gone.

My initial plan had been to photograph the Timothées against a pristine white background and interview each, but after the competition was banished from the park and decamped to nearby Mercer Playground, the Timothées were fleeting, just like the real one. I worked quickly, photographing the contestants on their way out, and the ones who'd come back, or arrived too late. There was no time for names or interviews so almost all were anonymous, in the same park where Diane Arbus had once photographed the dark edges of the 1960s.

The camera flashed and the Polaroids slid forth with their beautiful imperfections and unreliable colors. Afterward, as I thumbed through the pictures — most featured here — I realized this version of the event better captured whatever I'd set out to create on a Sunday afternoon in New York, so beautiful that it could break the heart of anyone with a pulse.

JONATHAN HOLLINGSWORTH
New York City, 2024

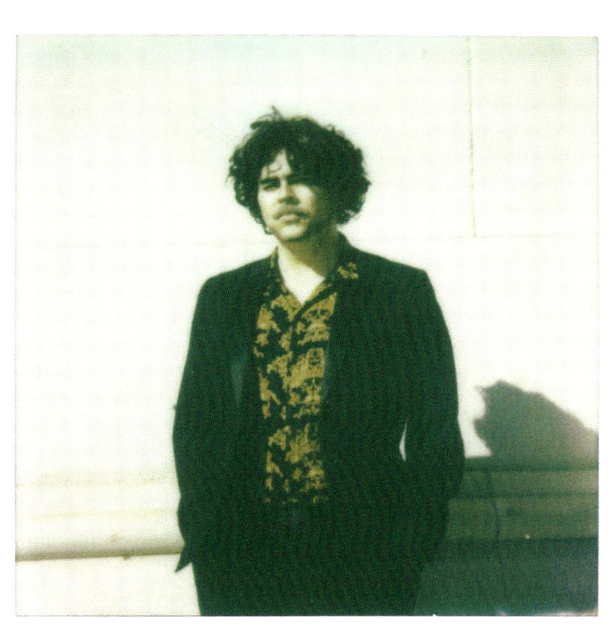

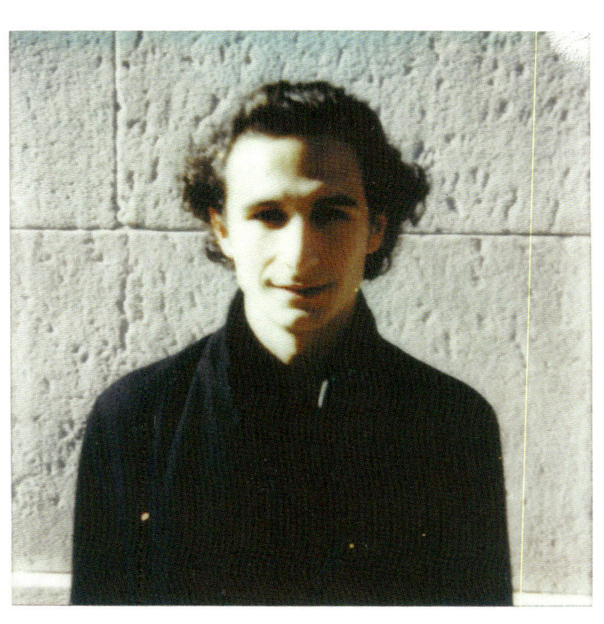

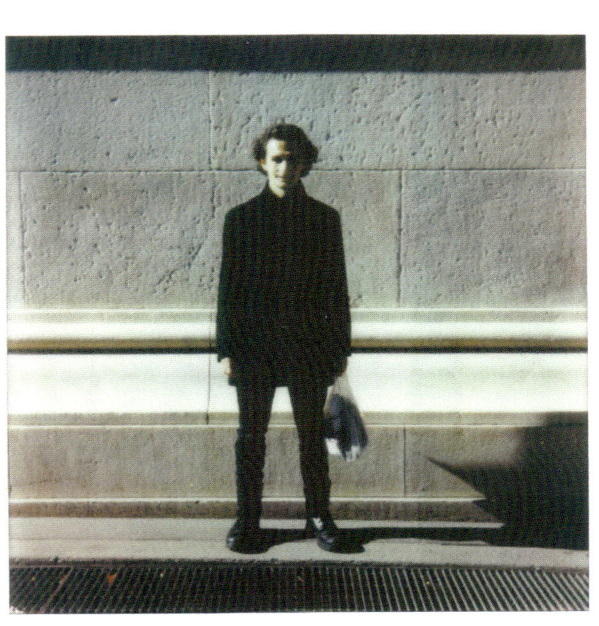

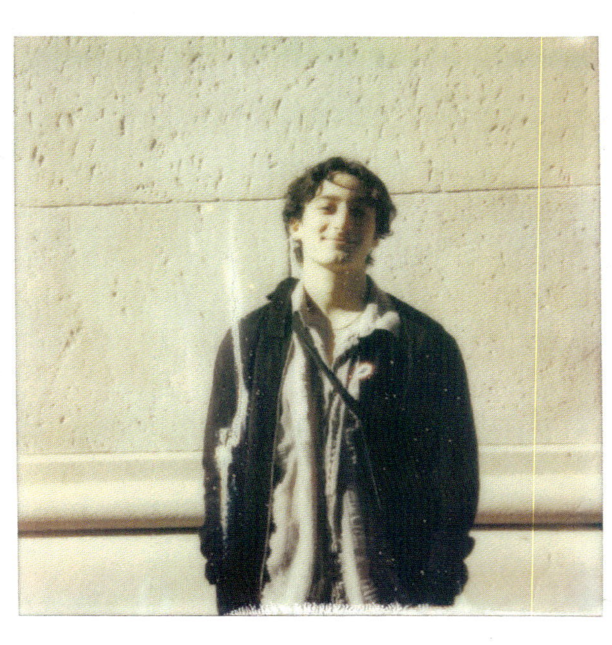

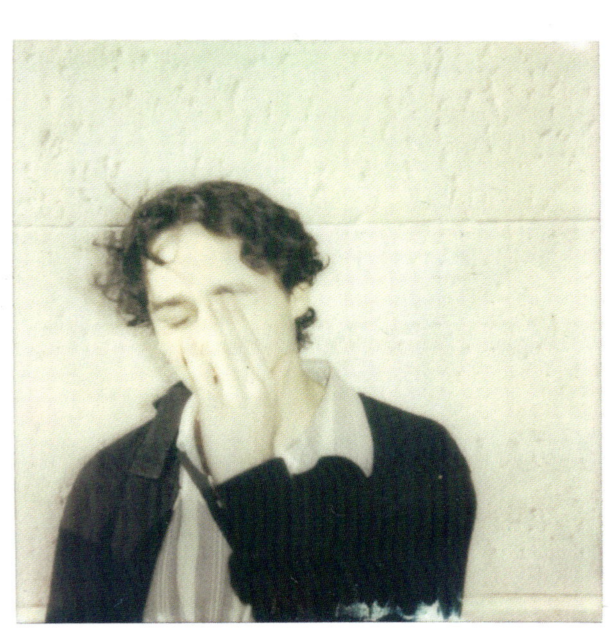

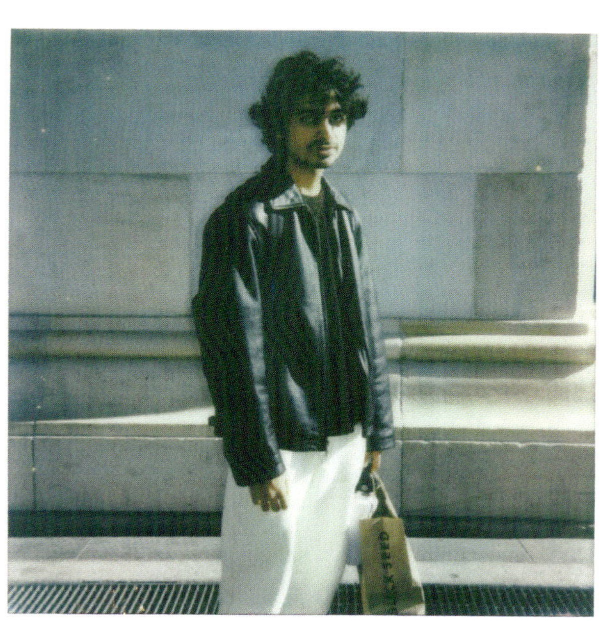

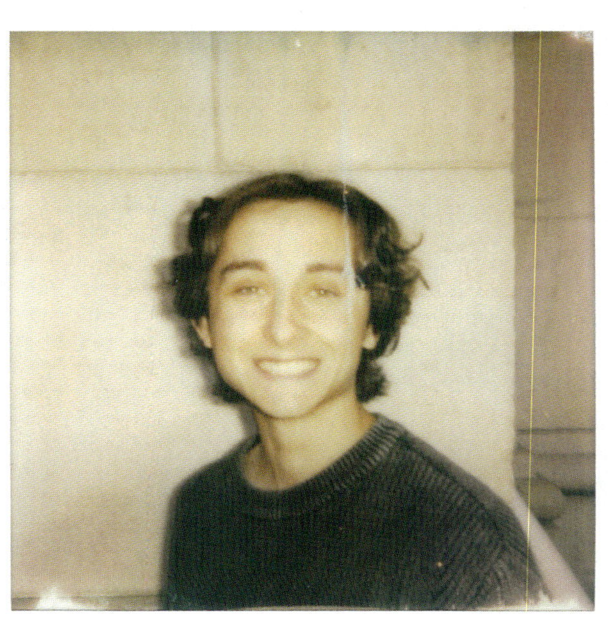

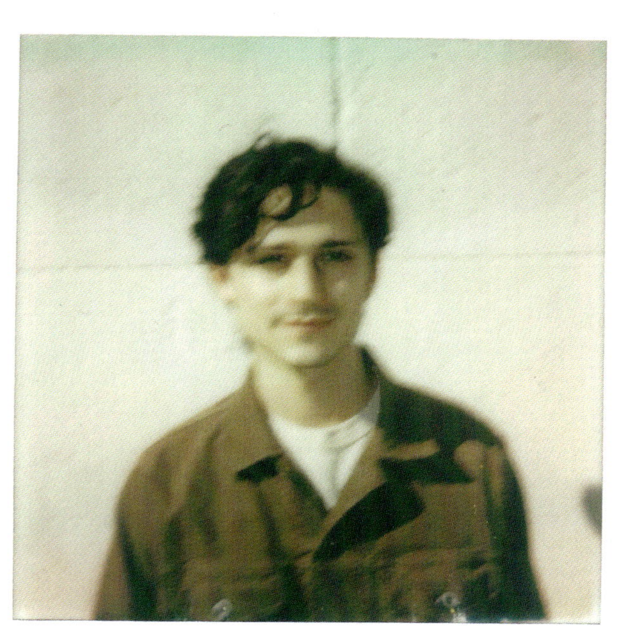

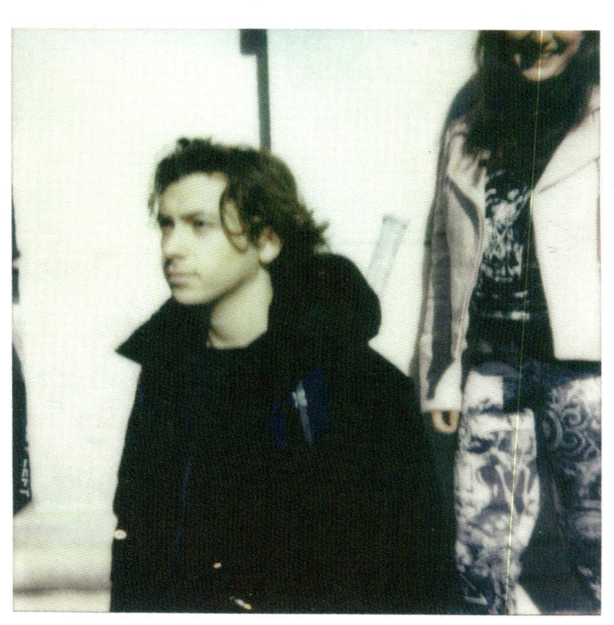

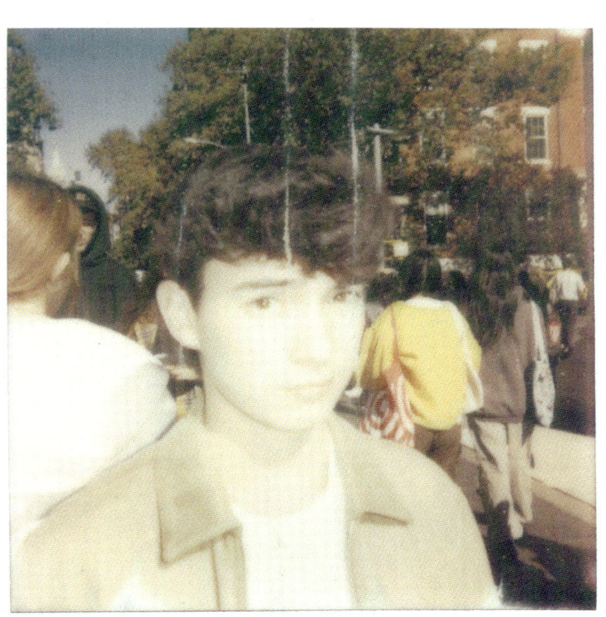

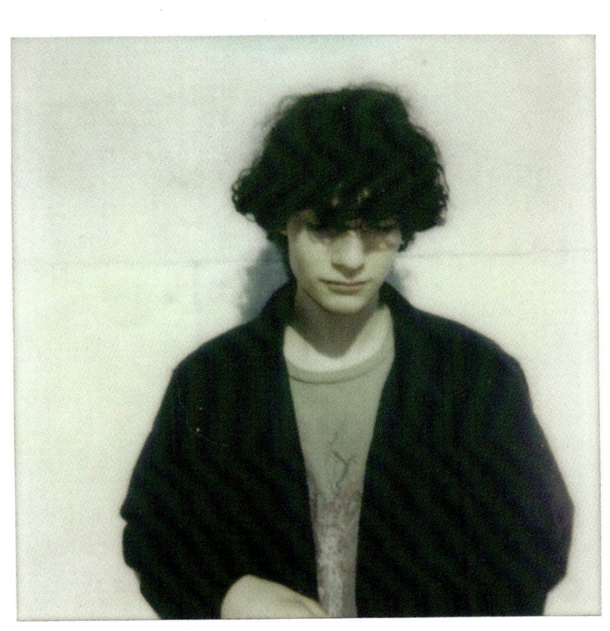

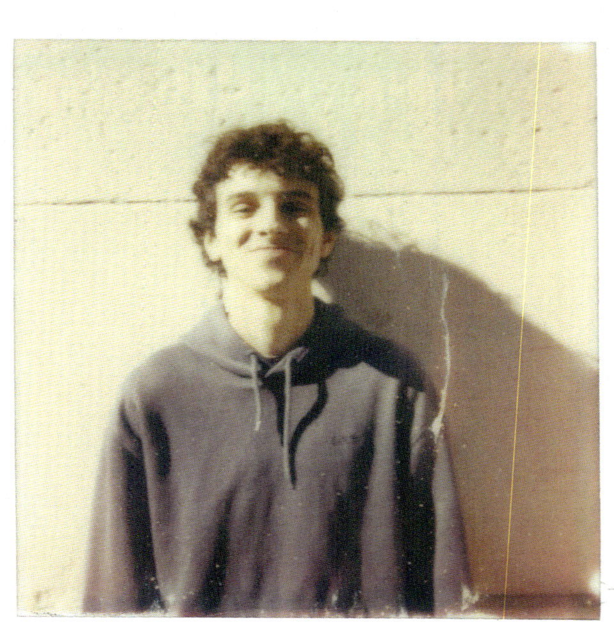

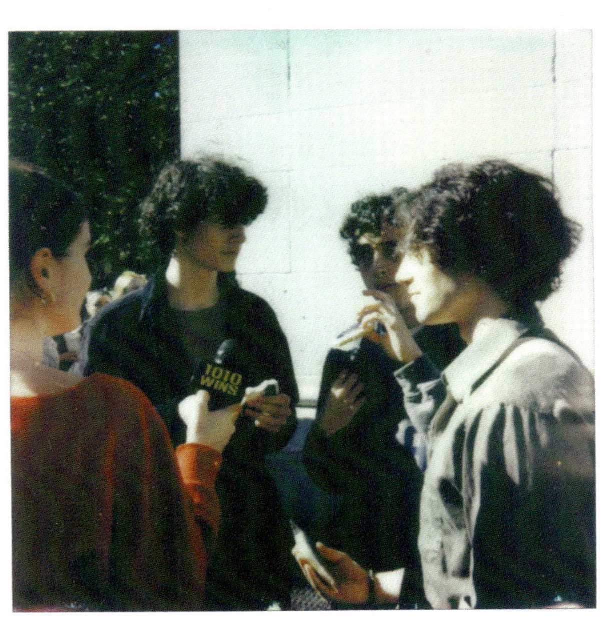

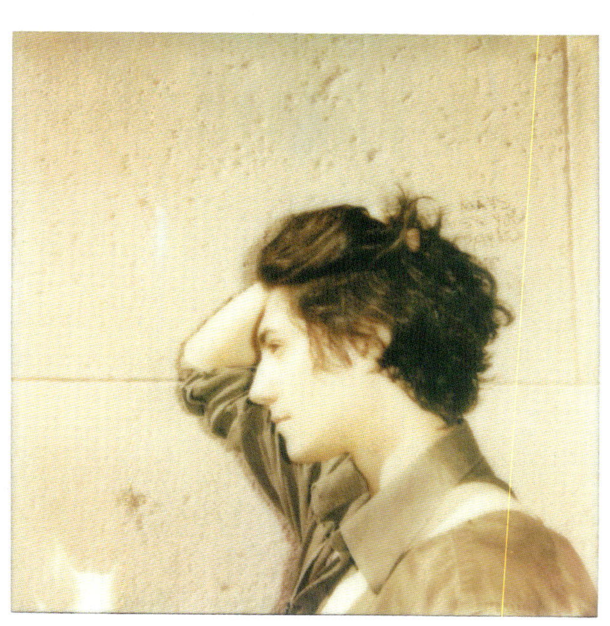

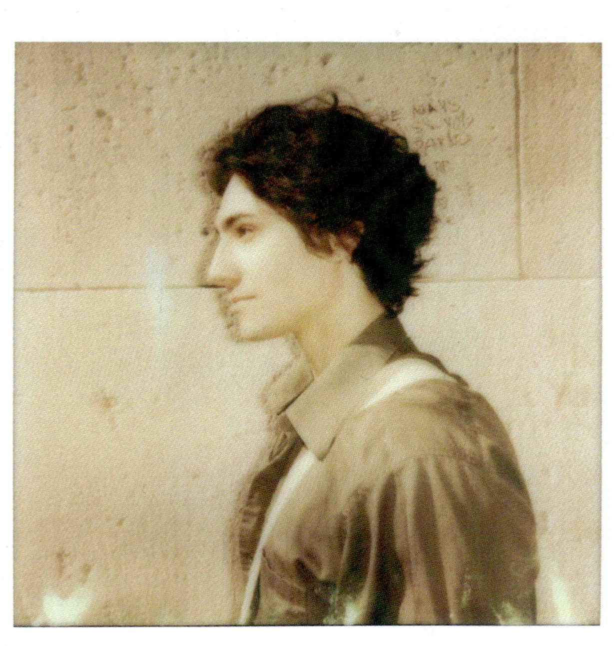

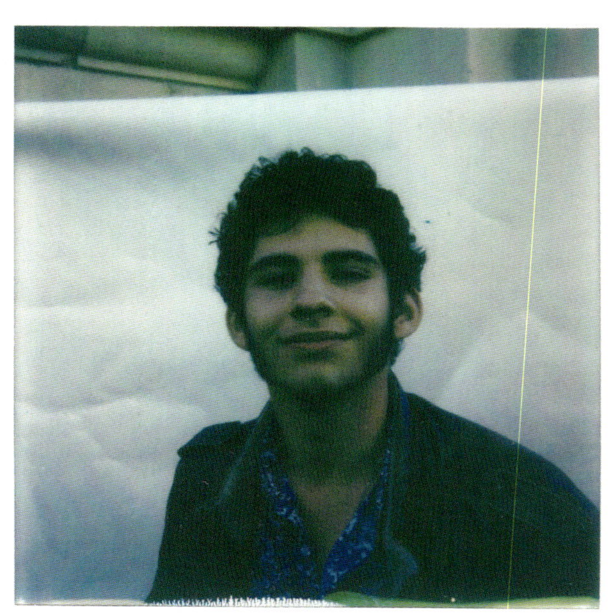

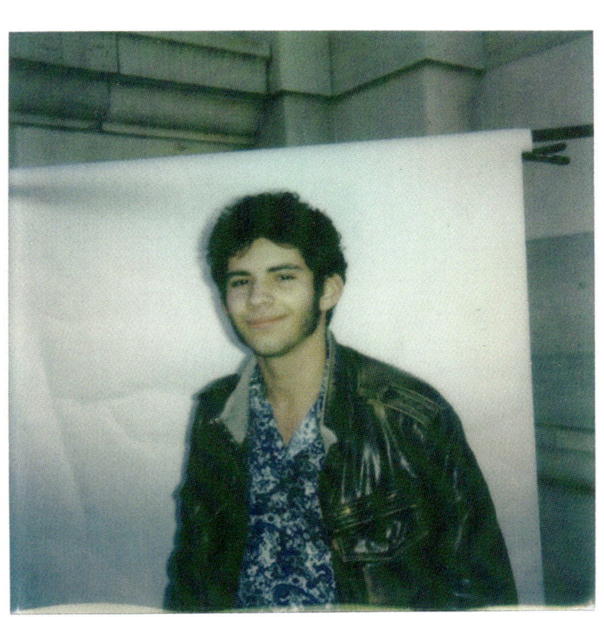

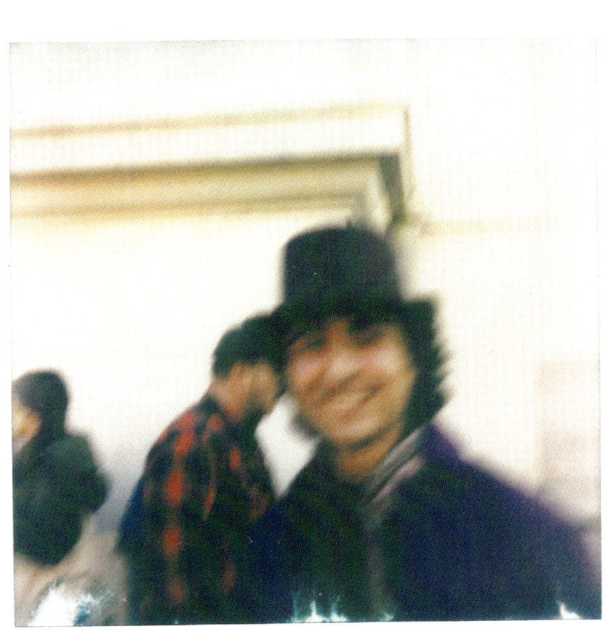

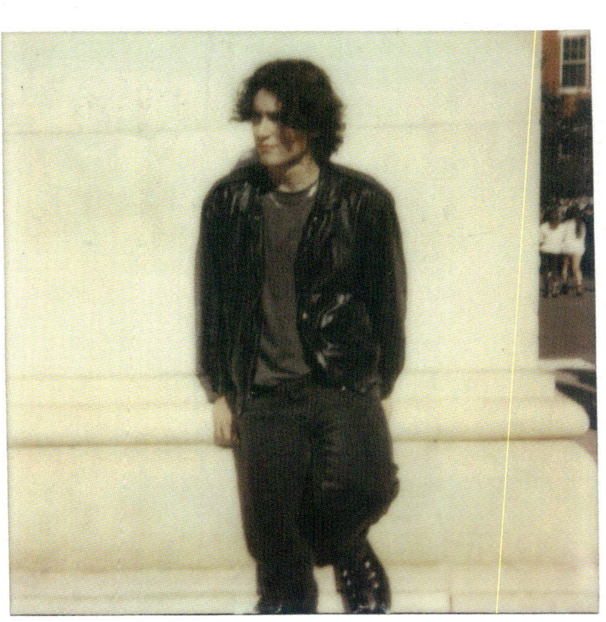

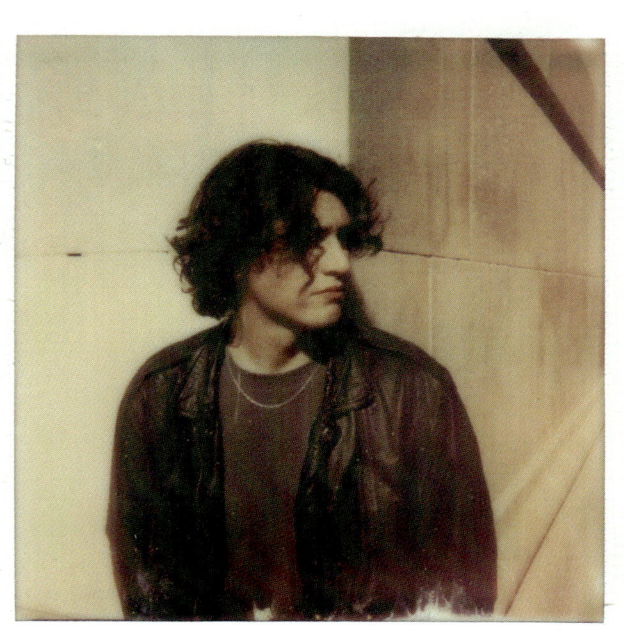

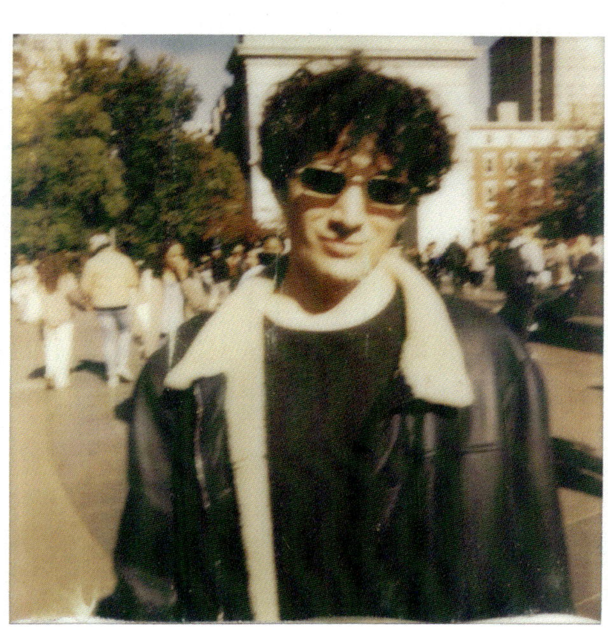

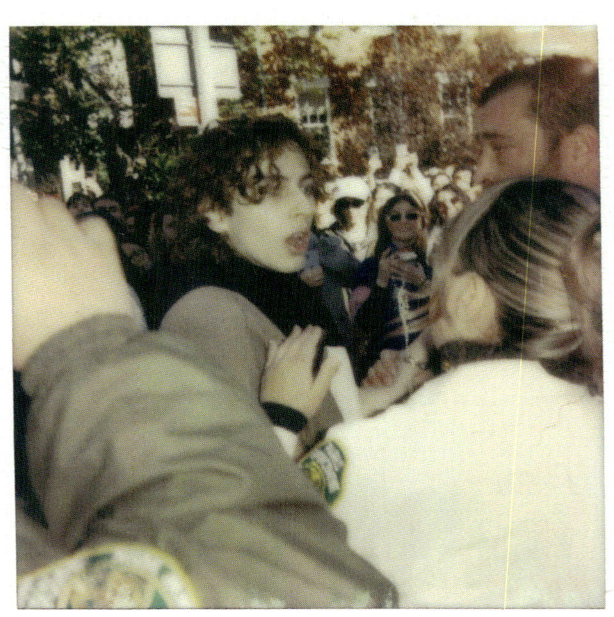

The Timothée Chalamet look-alike contest was exhilarating, lighthearted, and a day I'll never forget.

As I entered Washington Square Park, I got looks, smiles, and comments about having a great shot at winning. I won't lie: I was pretty anxious and excited entering the scene but everyone there was so nice and made it so much better.

When I got to the crowd, there were reporters, photographers, and TV networks that wanted to photograph and film me. I answered so many questions, I don't even remember everything I was asked. Then I worked my way to the center of the crowd with all the other contestants.

We took some photos and then the police broke everything up. They'd moved the competition down the street but I didn't even know because I got caught in a circle of cameras and people. I met some other contestants and we talked and took photos together. Even though I missed the crowning event, I wouldn't trade any of it for the experience I had interacting with so many great people.

In the end, Timothée did show up and took photos with friends I'd made at the competition which was awesome for them. Unfortunately, I only saw Timothée from a few feet away but I'm happy I still saw him. The experience showed the true greatness of the New York City community — and I learned what it was like to be Timothée Chalamet for a day!

REED PUTMAN, 21, Competitor [pictured on right]

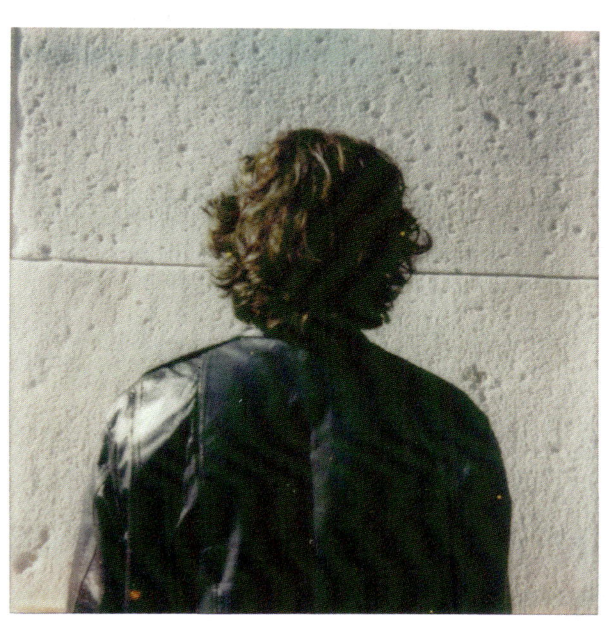

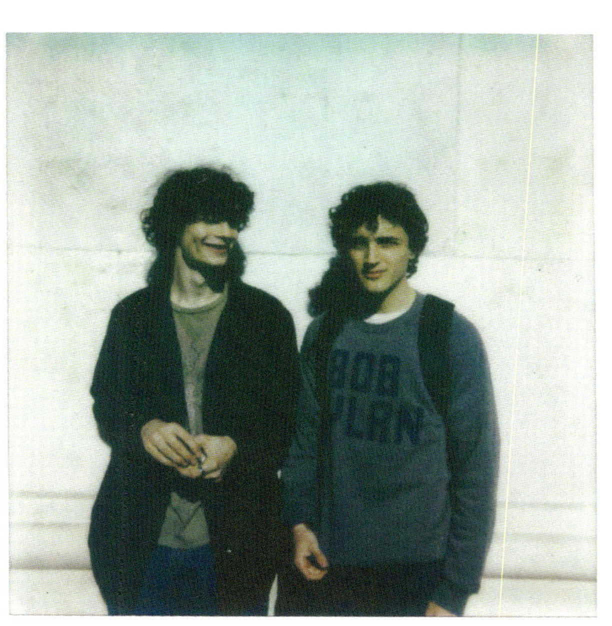
BOB
DYLAN

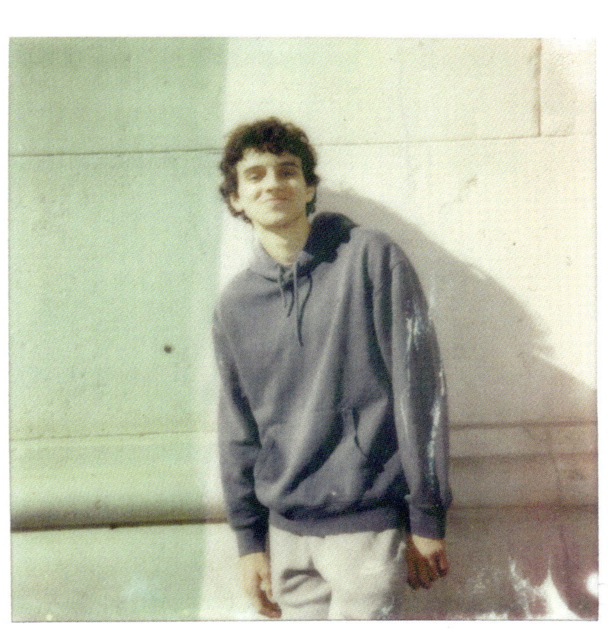

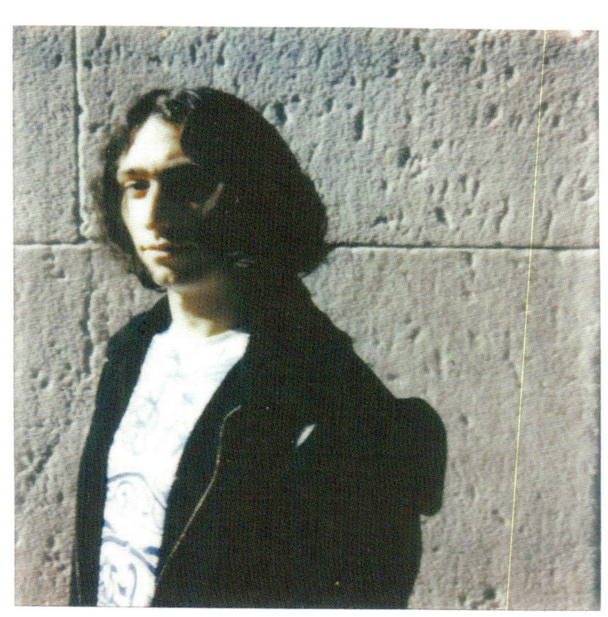

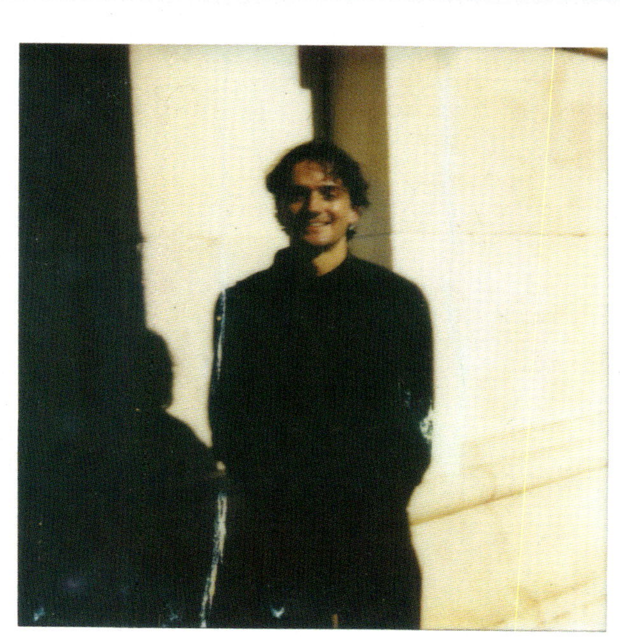

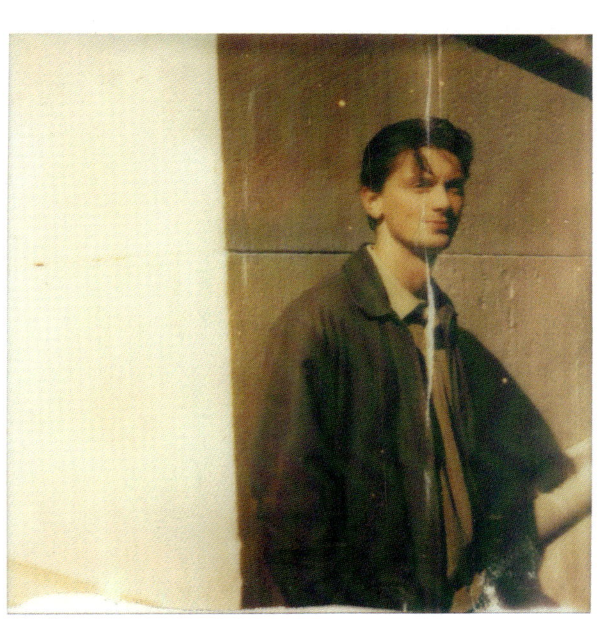

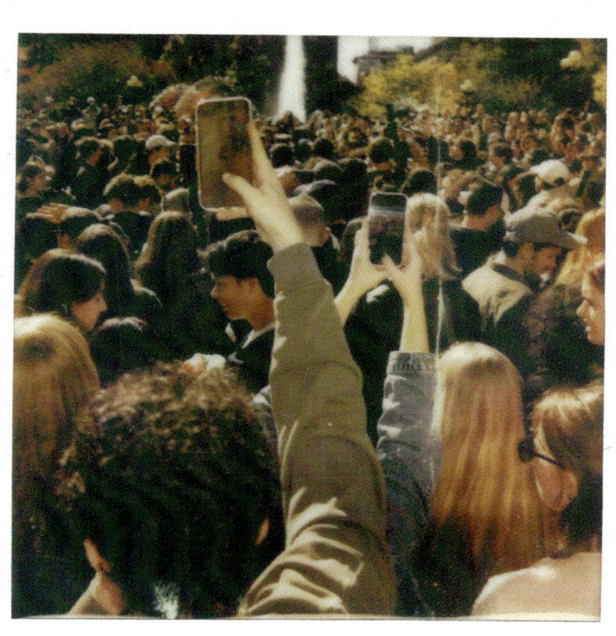

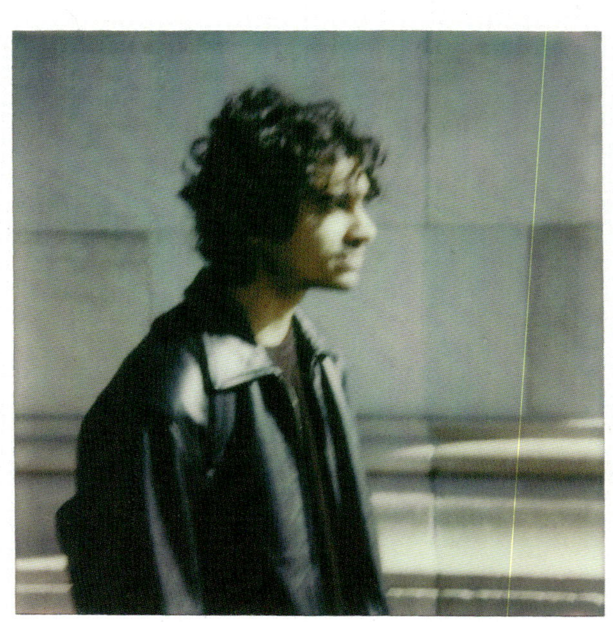

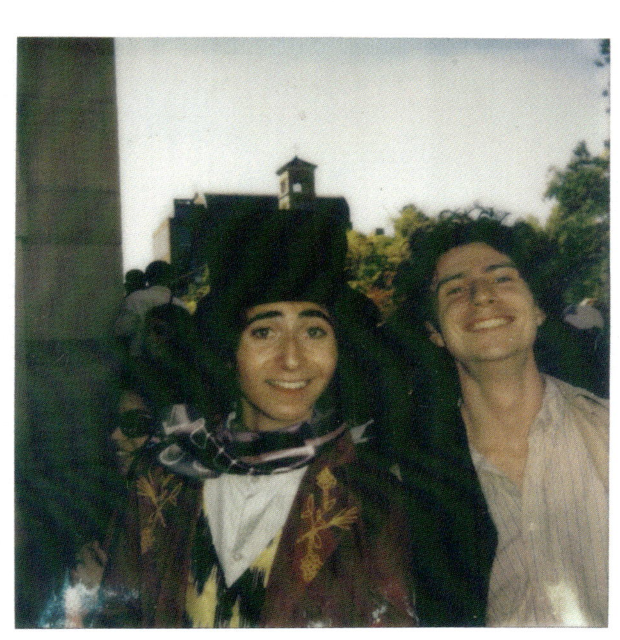

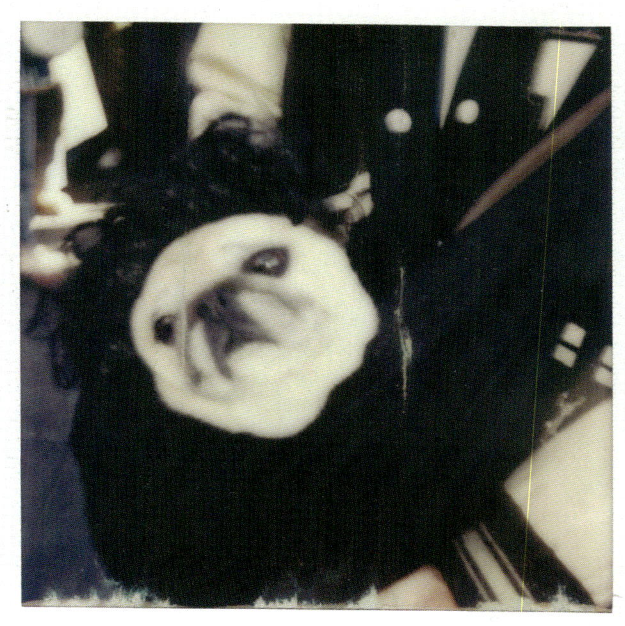

Jonathan Hollingsworth
Call Me Timothée:
The Timothée Chalamet Look-Alike Competition

Published by Blurring Books
BlurringBooks.com / @BlurringBooksNYC
Number 17 in the LSP Series

Photographs and text © 2024 Jonathan Hollingsworth

First Edition, First Printing of 350. There is a limited edition of 100 signed and numbered by the artist.

Jonathan Hollingsworth: Creative Direction and Book Design. Arlyn Eve Nathan: Typography. Sean Johnson: Production Management.

ISBN 978-1-963814-17-0
Printed in the U.K. in a CarbonNeutral® facility

Jonathan Hollingsworth is a New York City-based writer and photographer. His previous books include *What We Think Now: Young People's Response to the War in Iraq* and *Left Behind: Life and Death Along the U.S. Border.* He is the editor of *FLACO: The Owl Who Escaped Captivity and Won the Hearts of the World* (Blurring Books).

Special thanks to DB Burkeman, Sean Johnson, & Elliott Rogers (Blurring Books), David & Margaret Hollingsworth, Morgan Foxworth, Arlyn Nathan, Stefan Shanni, Anthony Po, Reed Putman, Julia Smerling and all the competitors who allowed me to take their picture.